# Los Alamos Mon Amour

SIMON BARRACLOUGH was born and raised in Huddersfield, West Yorkshire and now lives in London. He won the poetry section of the London Writers' Competition in 2000 and his work has appeared in *Poetry Review*, *The Manhattan Review*, *Time Out*, *Magma* and the anthologies *In the Criminal's Cabinet*, *Unfold* and *Ask for It by Name*.

# Los Alamos Mon Amour

## Simon Barraclough

*For Mark,*
*Lovely to meet you,*
*Simon*

**SALT**

CAMBRIDGE

PUBLISHED BY SALT PUBLISHING
PO Box 937, Great Wilbraham, Cambridge CB21 5JX United Kingdom

© Simon Barraclough, 2008

The right of Simon Barraclough to be identified as the
author of this work has been asserted by him in accordance
with Section 77 of the Copyright, Designs and Patents Act 1988.

Salt Publishing 2008

Printed and bound in the United Kingdom by Biddles Ltd, King's Lynn, Norfolk

Typeset in Swift 9.5 / 13

ISBN 978 1 84471 315 8 hardback

Salt Publishing Ltd gratefully acknowledges
the financial assistance of Arts Council England

1 3 5 7 9 8 6 4 2

*For Breda and Lorraine & in memory of Clive*

# Contents

# Acknowledgements

I'd like to thank the editors of the following magazines, in which many of these poems have appeared: *Cross Lines*; *Donga*; *Fin*; *LITRO*; *Magma*; *The Manhattan Review*; *nthposition*; *thepoem.co.uk*; *Poetry Review*; *Poetry News*; *The Poetry Worm*; *Rising*; *Stimulus Respond*; *Stride Magazine*; and *Time Out*.

'Brighton Restored' was published and illustrated in the book *Graphic Poetry* and 'Fusing the Braids' appeared in the anthology *In the Criminal's Cabinet*. 'Outlook Good' won first prize in the poetry section of The London Writer's Competition, 2000 and 'Nato e Morto' was a runner-up in the Yorkshire Open Poetry Competition, 2007. 'Corrie Sonnet' and 'The Open Road' were written for the British Film Institute commission, *O Dreamland*. Several of these poems also appeared in the pamphlets *Unfold* and *Ask for It by Name* (unfold press).

I'm also indebted to several poets for friendship, support and advice over the years: Helen Clare, Olivia Cole, Andrew Dilger, Luke Heeley, Hamish Ironside, Sue Stewart, Liane Strauss, Barbara Thimm, Roisin Tierney and, in particular, Isobel Dixon. Thanks also to Sonic Boom for permission to use Spacemen 3 album titles.

# Los Alamos Mon Amour

The second before and the eternity after
the smile that split the horizon from ear to ear,
the kiss that scorched the desert dunes to glass
and sealed the sun in its frozen amber.

Eyelids are gone, along with memories
of times when the without could be withheld
from the within; when atoms kept their sanctity
and matter meant. Should I have ducked and covered?

Instead of watching oases leap into steam,
matchwood ranches blown out like flames,
and listening to livestock scream and char
in test pens on the rim of the blast.

I might have painted myself white, or built a fallout room
full of cans and bottled water but it's clear
you'd have passed between cracks, under doors,
through keyholes and down the steps to my cellar

to set me wrapping and tagging my dead.
So I must be happy your cells have been flung through mine
and your fingers are plaiting my DNA;
my chromosomes whisper *you're here to stay.*

# Saturn on Seventh

I've been giving the miraculous a whirl
but what have I got? A stomach crammed

with cheap chimichanga, a shoulder-check
from Christian Slater and, though I don't know it yet,

a cloned credit card number. The Empire State
is a popsicle dipped in its Christmas reds

and greens. "Let's eat and drink ourselves
into hospital." The waitress only just

brought you round with ice-water fingers
on the cubicle floor between courses

and flaming, straw-melting cucarachas.
We came to celebrate this town

but dragging ourselves up Seventh Ave.
back to the peeling *Pennsylvania* room,

we sway wasted and weary past
stacks of Japanese *Playboys*, Brazilian

*Vogues*, battlements of L. Ron Hubbard
remainders, a trestle table over-stacked

with cheaply-stitched-together baseball caps:
all the naff globalised tat we've come

to expect from the greatest city on earth.
And then this charcoal-on-cardboard sign,

*See Saturn for a dollar*, and the giggling line
of clubbers where a homeless astronomer

has angled a prized and battered telescope
at a quarter of the sky to the right

of the Chrysler Building, which tonight
looks like it might have been piloted here

by Buster Crabbe. I toss a dollar in his cap
expecting nothing but empty night,

rest my brow against the rubber cup,
sealing out the street-level light

and there, in a black starless spotlight:
Saturn, as fat as a two pound coin,

fluxing with my pulse conducted through
the sensitive instrument, tilts its tipsy

rings towards Manhattan. I don't want to leave
its impeccable silence but you've paid

your money too and I step aside.
A random reveller asks me, "Did you see it?

Is it real?" and "Was it in colour?"
You take your fill and turn away, smiling.

We continue up the hill in silence,
our minds in parallel universes.

## Psycho

I heard at the heart of things
there's a massive black hole.
Gigantically coy but given away
by x-rays and the teetering
of attendant stars.

The blades of the Milky Way
Moulinex through space
as I shudder in your arms
and wait to be accused
of hyperbole again

because I saw the universe
drain down the plughole,
swirl back through the disc of your eye
and all that was lost was reborn
in the still silent face by my side.

# A Tall Story about a Pushover

A little knowledge can be a deadly thing.
The most glamorous woman of all time:
thief, liar, cheat; she was all of these things and he knew it.
Out of her curtained past came a man past all forgetting,
the most charming brute who ever scorned a lady,
the man who put the *man* in romance.
Strange, strange, their irresistible love; dark, dark, their inescapable
  fears.
Spies, playing the game of love and sudden death.
Three thousand miles of terror,
an ordinary necktie used with a deadly twist,
the guest who's dead on time,
a bomb plot, a killing, justice.
In his arms she felt safety; in his absence, haunting dread.
"You don't love me, I'm just some kind of wild animal you've trapped!"
For a moment he forgets he's a thief and she forgets she's a lady.
Who goes primitive first: a man or a woman adrift in an open boat?
See and hear it. Our mother tongue as it should be heard.
Crushed lips don't talk.
If a woman answers, hang on for dear life.
Somewhere, somewhere, there must be the right man.
You must see it twice.
*Suspense! Azione! Sorpresa!*
Don't give away the ending; it's the only one we have.

                                        *Thanks to www.imdb.com*

## Fusing the Braids

Three times a year you overhauled your hair,
firing the helical fuse that transformed
tightly-raked rows into electrical storms
of static and dandruff and ionised air.
Then, your black nimbus would radiate past
the edges of photos, pillows on beds,
reducing your face to a shrunken head,
leaving you other, untethered, distressed.
So for a weekend I became taboo
while expert fingers, with love, rebraided
the separate warring strands within you,
so I could return, all conflict evaded,
to pass a candle flame from tip to tip,
fusing hair and plastic, lip upon lip.

# The Open Road

What if colour film came first
and all these searing sunsets, curly copper mops,
pink-fringed parasols and gaudy frocks
were so much *blah* to an eye that thirsts

to watch an ashen rose unfurl,
see the charcoal sheen of a peacock's tail,
a seascape rolling in drab grayscale,
dun smudges on the cheeks of girls;

dancing flames of heatless brume,
rockets spraying asterisks of chalk,
greybells blooming on pallid stalks,
the world's flags starred and striped with gloom?

We wouldn't dress our hearts in motley threads
and fix the world in greens and reds,
projecting all the loves we said
we'd never leave but left for dead,

and might not glimpse the widening seam
between the separating reds and greens
of everything we'd thought we'd seen
on our memory's monitor or silver screen.

## Contacts

Jolts awake in the early hours,
eyelids crisp as courgette flowers,
turns towards the bedside blur
and sees the clock unusually clear.
4.50 a.m. with his contact lenses
Epoxied fast to his corneas.
Feet arch on tile as he peels back the lids
and pads at an iris with fingertip
but fails to find the lip between
the contact lens and all he's seen.
He's never known them so dried on,
must be the wine, the parching sun,
unless he's nudged them round the back:
two jellyfish in the lightless black.
Unfolds a hotel razor blade
from its envelope but he's not that brave
or desperate yet. Resumes the pincer
of thumbnail and index finger
and snags at last the stubborn seal,
with focused effort starts to peel
first one lens off and then the other
and lays them on a small hand mirror.
Unscrews their double-siloed case
to find them waiting in their place.
And on the mirror, torn asunder:
asquint Picasso, boss-eyed flounder.

# Unleashed

The years we kept it out the back—chained to the stake,
the firkin well within the reach of searching lips
and agile tongue; the years its oily fur grew rich
against the rain, and talons kept in check upon
the family tombstone propped aslant the drystone wall;
the years we fed it titbits from the table and dared
to pat its lengthening snout—were peaceful on the whole.

One restless night you saw the circle it had worn,
felt for the collar and finally unclasped our hold.
It pounced from the chain and the mist took its tracks.
So now we're blamed for the trampled crops, the upturned bins
and gutted sheep; there's been a sighting near the school
and at dusk the torches in the woods, the hue and cry,
the ancient howl, let us know that it's near,
though it may not know where it belongs or how to hunt or who
    to trust
or how to find its way back to us, even if it wanted to.

# Pike

Teriyaki tigering the golden
deep-fried flesh and a flask of hot sake
fuming like a factory chimney.

This china smoke stack takes me back
to failing mills and Warcar Reservoir:
the stagnant pond that used to juice them

before profit migrated East to the land
of synthetics, cheap worsted, cheaper labour.
The summer of *Jaws* and tucked-up legs,

invented verrucas, sliding Sunday nights
down the gullet of the weekend bath:
feeling like Quint kicking at teeth, puking blood.

Pike were our local great whites but we had
no pike nets, pike repellent, strychnine jabs,
no police chief or ichthyologist.

We had hunks of drystone wall, giant bobbins,
window gaffs, rafts of unhinged doors,
to protect us from the monstrous fish

that Ted Hughes himself might have reared
and delivered overnight on the back
of a flat-bed lorry.

We knew the tale of the kid who dived
onto a rusting Cortina,
swam to the cobbles and bound up

his intestines in a pinkening towel
and almost made it home. But we knew
the pike had done it, though we watched

the council land the dribbling chassis
with a crane. We dared ourselves
back into the green water,

rafting down the overflow when it rained,
stooping under child-sized Niagaras,
leaping from the millstone-gritty walls.

I never saw a pike in the res
or in a keepnet and now I have one
in a dish, spit-roasted on a skewer,

I'm sorry for its cooked-blind eyes,
seared-off fins, flaking muscle.
I take it apart with chopsticks.

## At Least

When I was a kid and the radio said:
"At least two hundred pilgrims dead . . ."
"At least twelve local fishermen drowned . . ."
"At least a thousand bodies found . . ."
"At least four casualties at the scene . . ."
I thought those southern voices mean
to sound relieved that the best attempts
of famine, war and pestilence
had at least some booty for their travails.
At least we weren't like that in Calderdale.

# Frigidaire

There was plenty of danger at home
but we sought more in the bowels
of textile mills, reservoirs,
rubbish tips. Swings over dams
turned gallows or put us in traction.
Unleashed Alsatians coursed us from
building yards where we bathed in silos
of multi-coloured sands, sliced ankles
nimbling over Slinkies of razor wire.

"I dare you." I watch his muddy calves
shuffle into the maw of the derelict
fridge. His shoes catch its rubber lip
and sneer it back. I grab the chrome handle
and whump it shut. It takes hours
for the rocking to stop, the chilling appeals
to peter out. Who'd have thought the tattered
seal would give such suck? Now it's dark, and there's
battenburg and *Sing Something Simple* for tea.

## Seroxat ®

Monday to Sunday, calendar-packed,
blister-wrapped; stepping stones
across a tinfoil plain that would jag
like metal on filling were it not
for these chalky Sherpas,
ushering me from and to my bed.
These are my morning-after, evening-before,
afternoon-during pills.

My parents led me deep into the woods,
so I shed a trail of white pellets,
only for the birds to snaffle them up
and leave me stranded. But they fell
from the sky as a thudding black rain;
I followed the broken birds home again.

## Celestial Navigation

Days adrift, waiting for the horizon,
waiting for a fix. The edge of the world
has been rubbed away by the clumsy thumb
of this depression. Isobaric whorls
weave an ancient tale of serial crimes
as the ocean takes the prints, rolled in and out
of the ink of this pitching sky.
My scattered charts have grown cataracts,
protractor and dividers sprout
crabby limbs and scuttle across the cockpit sole.
My sextant wilts, a spider plant starved
of light, starved of familiar sights.

I bailed my supplies overboard:
bloated macaroni and risotto
sloshed out to sea with my spices, herbs,
freeze-dried coffee and tea until there spread
from the stern a salty paella
of foamy food. I know I haven't drifted far
for I sometimes taste my old provisions
in the long drafts of water I drain from
my bailing bucket. Poseidon has so much
to offer, but I have no horses to drown
and I pray the ship's cat passed muster,
mewing bubbles as I held her under.

I sheeted her to the mast instead of reefing
in the mainsail and there she bids me,
claws rising and falling. The black Polaris
around which this vessel swirls under the sightless
cloud. She spits *S.O.S.* in the teeth
of the storm, but the radio mike
is a showerhead that spatters white static
and I don't know which way round S.O.S. goes.
I clip myself to the jackstay and curl
myself around the cable, wait
for this to pass, my spine against the mast.

## Modern & Obsolete

I'm eating in Addis, pretending to be a good Muslim.
Scooping begh wot with injera. Right hand only: messy business.

She gazes from across the street, wondering if I'm game
for a little postprandial? Or else she's hungry.

White vans and dark saloons slow to take a look but maybe
it's too early, too light? She stares down the hard-hatted

drivers of the Channel Tunnel Rail Link trucks. They slag
her by day, are more tender by night. Just a tad.

She's off, the tilting stride reminds me
of a Marx Brothers film: that business where Groucho

sets his watch by Margaret Dumont's pendulum gait. The plates
are cleared. An hour and twenty minutes and still no trade.

On the street I peer into the watchmaker's next door:
*Modern & Obsolete. Please ring the bell—half a minute*

*to get down.* The window a dashboard of mute dials, hands
gone, faces mouthing *Antimagnetic, White Star, Dogma,*

*Incabloc, Sundial, Chambord, Suisse. Any part supplied.*
*Mainsprings ordinary and unbraceable. Rough pinions*

*all sizes 6–14 teeth.* And on an index card
a Victorian dissection of a watch, each tiny cog and spring

sewn into place like the bones of a shrew or an exploded
map of the engine room of the human ear. "Need a girl?" Her face

suddenly behind mine. I leave too quickly, taking a flashbulb
memory of watch faces hovering where her eyes should be.

## Slippers and Spoons

After dad went,
a strange change in punishment.
Gone the check slipper
that coughed out its lining
with each rubber stroke
of the sole on behinds.

Now the wooden spoon
withdrawn from the drawer
whose cache of cutlery
had changed into weaponry.

With this in hand
she would chase me upstairs
and I spouted abuse
I would never have dared
in the days when my sins
were expunged by footwear.

# Giallo

Soho. Reading a book on grief
and a cocktail menu. Long Island Baby
blows me a kiss sticky with vodka,

Malibu, orange and cranberry juice,
her thighs a mile of white sand, her rock pool eyes
swarming with the many-limbed creatures

of desire. I long to join her
till I remember that Long Island foams
with sharks and the bones of whalers,

bobs with the drowned buoys of bloated bathers.
The cocktail shaker racket brings me back
to this sugar-ringed table and Soho Square in the rain.

It's been two years, but when the barmaid sees
my watering eyes, I say "My father just died."
Not fair on her, but then your death

has made me mean and I change my order
to a Rusty Nail. She nods but it's clear
this is a new one on her.

She's all Baileys and crème de menthe,
milk and cherries. Would you have gone for her?
Philandering was your one and only optimism.

Crushed ice and the flash of chrome
slash back my midnight horrors of you.
Black gloves, flesh mask, felt fedora. You stalk

me down Italian lanes and Yorkshire snickets,
lurk in my bedroom, shoes under the curtain,
ready with razor, garrotte, ice pick.

Before I wake, you dig your skewers
into my brain, teasing apart the folds and lobes,
the carpaccio of flesh and memory until

only the cocktail list can keep you at bay.
Two or three more and then, *mio caro*
*assassino*, you'll be in the can.

# The Death of Vito Corleone

DON CORLEONE: *I like to drink wine more than I used to.*
MICHAEL: *It's good for you, papa.*

*The Godfather*

Again with the oranges. Deadly zest.
Skin and pith for teeth he hunkers, growling.
They weave between vines of green tomatoes,
the bug sprayer spitting and clanking
in the little boy's hand.
                              I don't recall you ever
eating fruit. My memories grew in as they yanked
your full set. Drooling crimson in bed,
into the trifle bowl. Your moans:
wind through gappy rafters. Your plundered
mouth.
            He slugs another mouthful of vino
rosso, warns Michael of betrayals: Barzini
and the other families, the big shots.
*A man who does not spend time with his family*
*can never be a real man.*
                        I hate the fact
I know more about his death than yours. I chase his life
down through the vines until he finally keels
but it's only Brando bowing out,
mothballed mouth mumbling.

# For Sale

*(after Lowell)*

A draughty shoebox up on blocks,
Yorkshire Tea and terrier prints,
lived in just a year—
my dad's caravan at Sand Le Mer
was on the market the month he died.
Leaky, salt-lashed, anonymous,
Beatles and brass band LPs
warping in the yearlong must,
a copy of *Emmanuelle*
and framed royalties from Radio Three.
His second divorce beached him here
and he couldn't support his own weight,
and his dog gnawed the fur
from its paws for a year
and had to be given away.

# The X-ray Room

This is small beer, at worst a chipped orbital bone.
But the silhouette of crown and brow—
black as space—thrown against the metal plate,
the segmented camera craning back to shoot

its payload of photons through my skull, fill me
with projected fears. It's not this injury
but the ones to come: shadow puppets figured
through the lamps of my eyes, leaning on crooked canes,

batting at murderous crows, dancing for Satan
under full moons, shedding their skin like clothes
and stepping down into their graves at dawn.
On a sticker designed to help kiddies through

the ordeal, a fading teddy bear brandishing
balloons says *I've been brave!* Maybe I have.
For the next headshot I lie back on the bench.
My first thought is to hand back the black leaden mat

she places so carefully over my crotch.
"All clear," she beams minutes later. I'm almost sad
to leave so intimate a place. I hurry past
an open door where a CAT scan machine lies in wait.

# Retuning St Paul's

*(after Spacemen 3)*

*For all the fucked up children of this world*
*we give you*: St Paul's on retuning day.
*Taking drugs to make music to take drugs to.*
Once a year the gargantuan organ
gets a good going-over. Each note held down
for thirty minutes or so. Building,
reverbing, pulsating from the nave
up spiralling stairs, from Whispering
to Golden Gallery. I can't see him
but I like to think the tuner is jamming
bone-handled knives between the keys, yanking
each ancient stop to full whack, smearing
red gums with coke, snorting smoke from the censer,
Phantom of the Opera, pre-Reformer.

# Abductees

I've read their accounts and I sympathise
with those, in the night, in their homes, by surprise,
taken from children, husbands, or wives
and living in fear for the rest of their lives.

Who lose an hour here, an evening there,
barrelling home from God knows where,
who awoke doing seventy in the car
and found in the shower a tiny new scar.

Minuscule holes drilled into the molars,
polygonal bruising between the shoulders,
nosebleeds and blackouts and nightmares by day
and a pregnancy that just went away.

They never fetched me (although I prayed)
in their rainbow ships but I often strayed
to the brow of the moor where the stars were clear
and the crisp air crackled with something near

from so far away from that wintry town,
come to thaw the peat through and settle down
on Pole Moor or West Nab or on Holme Moss,
but no shadows joined mine upon the frost.

# The York Realist

Above the chatter of cutlery,
the scritch of tine on scallop shell
and finger-snap of *grissini*,
you illuminate this tablecloth

with gloss and marginalia
from your recent lecture
in Florence. Early verse drama.
*The Life and Repentaunce*

*of Marie Magdalene.*
I'm crass enough to picture you
fleeing Hannibal Lecter
across the Piazza del Duomo

but smart enough to drown
my thoughts in wine and weight my tongue
with plump folds of bream you offer me.
Further back: to Lindisfarne,

*The Mystery Plays*, how the Pinners
nailed Him up and the Butchers
rolled the stone, but we couldn't recall
the guild that dug Him out again.

I've nothing to add but a tip
to the salver, nothing to do
but down the last sediments.
Your flight to Vancouver pounces.

The crescent of hotels, the kiss
I wish I'd held, your ageless Egyptian locks.
Quick march to Holborn, Epping train,
whitening toothpaste, winding sheet.

# Long Haul

### 1

"We have no more *chilled* chardonnay," she hisses.
Another lunch that unravelled past
our nine-to-five commitments, dusk,
now midnight. Our coats and keys
are in the office. If we could walk
we'd retrieve these clues but we're falling
through the restaurant and onto Cheapside.
City types tut as they step over us.
We roll in rain, my face rucked up
against the tread of a Porsche's tyre,
your hand already in my flies.

### 2

Ninety-six Oregon Zinfandel,
Windows on the World. Calamari
from Maine, seared swordfish in cep
and champagne sauce. Just two years ago
but the website has slipped from Google,
seventy-nine staffers are missing. Who knew
we were dining at the epicentre?
Well, someone should have. We joke
with the married couple who've ordered
the exact same meals as us, pretend
you're not engaged, I'm single.

3

Hot sake, green tea in The Tao,
Bow Lane. Chopstick contests.
I handle my salmon skin maki
pretty well but you shake your head,
tweeze a sole flying fish egg
that squints free of your lacquered sticks
and down your blouse.
At the base of The Monument,
CCTV lenses unblinking,
I find the faint spoor of that egg
and track it with my tongue.


4

You've a novel under your belt—
no slur intended—but back then
you were still on short stories.
Hours in Barnes and Noble
choosing the best anthology,
rewarding ourselves with pitcher
after pitcher of margaritas.
"No sign of it," they said the next day.
Was it my disdain for prose,
or the thought of your fiancé
put you on the plane with no replacement?

5

Your midnight message brings me here,
leaning into the gales, worrying
that jet-lagged, afraid of terrorists,
you've forgotten the clocks went back.
The heavy doors of the Royal Festival Hall
blow open and quiver on the crests
of gusts from the sepia river.
An air lock forms in which the second call comes.
"Can't get away . . . feel as bad as you . . .
surprise party . . . husband." Nothing for it:
buy some Berryman, find a bar, pass out.

# The Dream Song of Saddam Hussein

Huffy Hussein hid      the day,
unappeasable Saddam sulked.
I see his point,—a trying to put one over.
It was the thought that they thought
they could *do* it made Saddam to Tikrit and away.
And now he's come out will he talk?

All the world like a sleeping partner
once did seem on Saddam's side.
Then came a departure.
Thereafter nothing fell out as it might or ought.
No way that Saddam, pried
open for all the world, could have survived.

What he has now to say is a long
wonder the world can bear & be.
Once in a date palm tree I was glad
all at the top and I sang.
Hard on the land wear the Humvees
and empty grows every gaol.

# Son

Came back from Kabul all wrong.
Didn't stick around for too long
after that. Left the army and his mum
asking where her boy had gone.
Sold his kit and caboodle for a song
and worked the Pacific around to Hong Kong.
Took a postcard of Dunfermline along.
Can't speak of those things in a foreign tongue
so he's teaching a PADI course in Haiphong,
sleeps with his new wife and a handgun.

## Awake Again

Crosstown bus climbs the camber of Manhattan.
A man in a Kangol cap sways from a handle,
squeezing a Yorkshire Terrier as close as bagpipes.
The Queen Mother asks, "Are dogs a status symbol?"
The tiny chicken-boned creature trembles.
She's all in black. I say, "I'm sorry for your loss."
She tells me not to worry; that death allows her
to travel unattended. As I pass her to alight,
I see towers through the gauze of her veil.
She kisses my cheek with lips like Fall
and whispers, "You're a good soldier."

# Goodbye Radio City

Forget the famous neon venue,
    New York is not a radio-friendly
        place. From the plane, a circuit board bristling

with transistors, capacitors, soldered
    avenues, the Empire State tracking
        across the green dial of Central Park,

fizzing through the channels of a hundred
    jabbering neighbourhoods. Nearer ground
        the radio waves smash and shatter

against concrete impedimenta.
    Snatches of song, Yankees games, *Nobody*
        *Beats The Wiz!* career and try to stay whole.

If radio thrives anywhere it's in
    cabs, cop cars, meat wagons, fire trucks,
        meshing the grid of lives, accidents

and catastrophes. But pictures dominate.
    The North Tower's mast only budded four
        radio transmitters, the rest TV.

Donald DiFranco, Steve Jacobson, William Steckman,
    Bob Pattison, Gerard Copolla, Isaias Rivera
        were tending their antennas that day,

enabling the city to watch, on cable,
    from satellite, their imminent closedown.
        Now there's a new rescue mission

out at Alpine, New Jersey, where
     Edwin Armstrong, father of static-free FM,
         stepped out of his 13th floor apartment

window in 1954.
     An overcrowded Empire State sees
         the transmitters leaving the island:

out of the centre, away from the heat,
     the dust, the fear. And anyway, everyone says
         you get the best views of the city from here.

## Protecting St Paul's

Since the shit hit the fan we're on Brown Alert.
Guaranteed a bobby in a box
near a dragon, preserving The City.
With his *I-Spy* of Anarchists and Irish
in suspect vans, he now peels his eyes
for Al Qaeda foot soldiers, anthrax mailers,
C-4 body warmers. An extra guard
slouches between escalators underground,
guiding the better-looking women onto
the moving stairs with his eyes and watching
their backs as they rise. Despite all this,
I swear I heard the approaching drone,
saw a wing tip shear off the eggshell dome.

## Buffy is Leaving Tuscan House

It's time to let her go, the green-eyed blonde
who for years has watched over my sleep,
dusting vampires while I hid beneath sheets.
No monster ever curled its claw from underneath
my sock drawer that didn't meet a swift demise,
or slide the helter-skelter back to Hell.
But not for her the building's rubbish chute.
My umpire parleying the crease between
the boundaries of nightmare and dream,
wearing hats and scarves; my running medals
hanging from her suntanned, cardboard neck.
I'll divest her of these youthful things and fold her
flat, take her for once under my wing and to the lift.
"Ooh, I say what have you got there?" I blush.
"It's an old gift I've outgrown." "Ain't she lovely, though.
How can you chuck her out?" "It's hard but it's time."
She needs her new adventures and I need mine.

# The Approach

I'm drinking in truant time with Jerome K. Jerome,
pints of 6X and my local's jukebox of punditry and pop.
Regulars hunch around the fireplace lunchtimes to reprise
their affections for The Gunners, Spurs, The Hammers;
compare their carbon footprints; lament the last of the Krays;
berate the Brit-Art wankers from Hoxton with their timber-framed
spectacles who swarm to openings in the gallery upstairs.
Talk turns to the century's greatest films. They tout Hitchcock
and Capra, "Get Carter", "Larry of Arabia", and one cinephile
suggests, "2001: A Space Holiday" to murmurs of cautious approval.
"Is that the one with the monkey suits and Rigsby out of
	Rising Damp?"
I leave George, Harris and Montmorency struggling
with canvas and close my eyes, my palm around my pint.

# London Whale

Two journeys you took in your last two days:
the first unwisely swimming west and then
carried unluckily east in a poor sling,
a small red watering can barely wetting
the wrongheaded brow that saw fit to squeeze
you through the gate line of the Thames Barrier.
Just another morning commuter
touching in or out with an Oyster card.
If you were heading for work, what strange job, this?
Unbriefed ambassador, curious key
to some ancient chamber flooded with guilt,
or love, or the rattling blades of that bad old trade
which it seems never touched you. Why here and now,
you smiling stranger? Do they sing about the bones
in the old museum? Did you *have* to chance it?
Look how sentimental you make me;
we're a city of visitors, you see.

# Converting St Paul's

"There's no such thing as a Protestant cathedral."
We're sitting in Balls Brothers' garden, gazing
at the pigeon-grey dome of St Paul's, which,
in its ample folds of Portland stone,
looks pretty convincing. "So what do you make of that?"
Pause. "It's just a hump-backed monument
to the Empire." I think of Wellington and Nelson,
the Falklands War, the hidden chapel
where OBEs can get hitched. She may have a point.
I swirl my pinot grigio in the bowl
of the fine-stemmed glass, like they taught me
at Vinopolis. The dome that might have dwarfed
St Peter's genuflects, submerged in the heat haze
of pale wine as if bathed in Roman sunshine.

## In Bocca al Lupo

The airport has closed, the trains are frozen
    to their tracks, the Alps cold-shoulder me and drop

a winter's weight of snow into my lap. With my grappa headache
    I lounge on grammar books, flicking channels

and finding a rare programme free of hot pants, toupees,
    wet t-shirts. On a map of old Europe I watch the habitats

of the grey wolf shrink. Shot, poisoned, built
    out of existence and fucking up its DNA with the feral strays

of the towns padding into the countryside.
    Mist bristles its coat against the French windows

and I'm off again, making a little sleep
    to while away this time away from you while

the hotel car park disappears, the footprints of the *Bergamaschi*
    are snuffed out for the day. You slip through a distant door,

your basket laden with *casoncelli*, yellow cakes with marzipan larks
    pecking at the sponge, and a flask of local red—

for you when you tire, for her as she births into your snow-white
    hands. The television wakes me to static blue

and I see you at the window, face floating in the mist, nails
    scratching the glass, red lips fuller than of late.

Your basket melts a patch of stone on the step,
    stirs with the life inside.

## Italian Verb Drills

A dozen dancing declensions to partner.
Unfailingly, I choose the wrong ending:
decoupling from the remote past
to embrace the simple future,
which dissolves in my clasp,
leaving only an opera glove behind.

# Titanica

What is this free-floating, free
radical, skulking near the hull
of her name? That lowercase 'a',

Hardy's "sinister mate" straking beneath
the waterline, tearing the word
inside out, dousing the boiler rooms

with significance. This lone letter tugs
and pilots her to the lightless port
where bowler hats, playing cards, luggage

tags, soup spoons and hair slides glow
and spectre the sunken gloom. Beacons
for our homing instinct, the never-ending

search for our dead. Salvaged now, curated
under glass, voiced by actors, audio-guided,
reconstructed, this suffocated

memorabilia joins other '———a's:
Americana, Judaica, Australiana . . .
in polite, sensitively lit, mausolea.

# Wearing St Paul's

*Don't you wish you had a skirt? I feel so sorry for you in those hot pants.*
MARILYN MONROE

I scale these stairs for the sense of grandeur,
don the ball and cross as a kind of mitre,
thread the Golden Gallery about my waist,
hooking into my Sunday Best of faith,
embracing a change of heart and gender
as the dome spills out its slate-blue organza.
I stride through town in my giant skirts,
trailing their fringes through the London dirt.
Like subway draughts in *The Seven Year Itch*,
the winds of modernity gust and hitch
the hoops right over my head, revealing
canon and clergy hurriedly fleeing
down to the docks to sail back to Rome
to cling to the hem of that wider, safer, dome.

## Exploratory

The great white shark will nudge a curious bite,
turn tail if it tastes fibreglass, neoprene or human meat.
You kissed me,
gauging watertightness, whether the seal would withstand
tidal pressures.
Flitted down the murk of a London night;
me with slippery handfuls of tissue loss,
pinching unknittable seams,
convulsing in your wake.

# Apologia

She rarely felt the need to apologise.
When she did, her contrition met with
exonerating pouts, enveloping hugs,
the nipping in the bud of any grudge.
I tried apologising to her once
after one of my turns, full of Armagnac,
spinning off the comet tail of Seroxat
or some such serotonin-shooting star.
No fear. Wouldn't budge. Got nothing.
Email after email, Interfloral
interventions, quarter-hourly texts;
she would not forgive or forget. So,
her larynx remains bruised, her dining table
smashed, her kitten's head the wrong way round.

# Withdrawal Method

Weird to be
undoing
all this.

Unplanting
every kiss,
gagging
each morsel
of every meal
into this
napkin,
curling
your cells
from under
my nails,
gouging
your voice
from my ears.

Did you ever
see *Poltergeist*?
There a man
tears his face
from his skull
in the bathroom.

I cram
lips teeth
gums hair
into
the overflow.

# Brighton Restored

Buckingham Road's solitary greengrocer
has let his shop go. Opposite our too-hasty
love nest, his window once shone
with pineapple, marrow, plantain and pumpkin
so pleased with themselves they might split.
Over twelve summers the window darkened,
thickening—an unrestored canvas—
from Matisse to Max Ernst. A wilderness
of overreaching bulbs, stray shoots,
liquefied tubers and greens. A thousand
generations of houseflies catacomb
the empty shelves.

I look back at our old double bedroom,
still curtained at noon. What rot has taken there?
What plates of unfinished takeaway
are stinking under the bed?
Are there piles of dress shoes gone to must
from the broken shower that blistered the walls?
Is another summer couple playing
at monogamy, choosing children's names,
calling psychiatrists out at dawn
to bring the foggy pills
that clouded my eyes and burned my skin
in winter sun?

I walk the route I used to run on nights
your eyes shone demon-bright in that room
so dark by day, too light at night for sleep.
Once, poisoned by paracetamol,
another time fleeing from your body
and the silken cicatrix where your "clumsy
African navel" bulged for the first five years
of your once-tropical life; the wound that spread
and mottled your torso with scarring
words of ancestral accusation;
and your fingers, ringed with African gold
from the "Prince" you fucked on your last trip home.

Becalmed by Palace Pier I wonder how
I let this drizzling town commandeer my twenties?
The West Pier, once reft, now pinioned
to the shore with steely new struts, no longer
speaks of gaps, of obliterated nights,
of a missing week in a hospital gown.
It is being restored. And maybe Alf's
Greengrocers will find a new lease:
reborn as a local estate agent,
Vespa dealer or Carphone Warehouse.
I know this: I won't be signing tariffs,
test driving scooters or viewing flats.
I'll be unmooring this town from its piers
and letting it drift.

# Christmas at the School of Psychological Medicine

is a dish of Quality Street
with all the purple nut and caramels removed.
The drinks machine, like a seaside mayor,
stands stiffly in its tinsel regalia,
single teat dripping Kenco and Fanta.

*What on earth am I doing here?*
Portuguese men o' war float near the ceiling,
far from their spawning pools at Woolworths
and injection-moulded mistletoe
droops from the Saneline emergency number.

She's late. I sneak a piss in the Staff Only toilet,
return to the landslip of magazines:
nothing here newer than three years old.
We're not to be trusted with currency,
but *Top Gear* and *Celebrity Brides* can't hurt.

For the first time in weeks I may have something
to share, not just stare at her stylish boots,
the green pipes of her countrified corduroys,
before drifting off on the couch.
"Today, you let me see the baby you."

I dreamt in the hospital ward that my aunt
slid her hands inside my gown and pinched
a slub of flesh from my navel, spooled my gut
around her fingers, snapped it free
and dropped it in her knitting basket.

The holiday traffic is holding her up.
*So leave a little earlier for God's sake.*
*Try taking the tube. I'm here and I'm the one*
*whose life is* . . . better to grout my rage
with toffee between the molars. Chew it over.

# Soloist

### 1

A new solo piece: first cornet, last post.
No theatre lights or hothouse tuition
to hoist me to the sacrificial C
high above my darling crotchets
that cleave to the foot of the stave.

You drank with the conductor and propelled me past
my peers, from third-cornet bit-part blower
to spotlit soloist, where I screeched and brayed
my *Onward Christian Soldiers*, marching as to war.

Caught on cassette for post-pub suppers,
the laughter climbing the stairs to my room.

### 2

The answer-phone tape filled up.
My sister twice, five times my mum,
an uncle, an aunt and then, at the last,
a new widow with it all to arrange.

### 3

On your big day you're quite the dandy.
Lying in state, more dapper than in life,
this crematorium chapel your Kremlin.

I once borrowed *Leninism Under Lenin*
with your library card to scare you,
to get back at you after you left,
and would stare impassively in your new flat,
before shutting the tome and reaching
for Einstein's *Principle of Relativity*.

Melomaniacal to a fault, you would *tut*,
continue to catalogue classical tapes.
Maybe Solzhenitsyn would do the trick
and make you feel blinkered, narrow, thick.

But there's a slide show of you in the States
I would beg to be shown as a boy.
A carousel-crumpled case in the loft,
hinging on stickers from your tour
with the Coldstream Guards—
Oklahoma, Albuquerque, Tallahassee,
Chicago, Seattle, Hawaii,
Dallas, Las Vegas, NYC—
before family, in the land of the free.

And when I made it to the Empire State,
I thought of you, skinny lad, gazing uptown,
world and euphonium at your feet
and the childhood burn on your cheek
the shape of Manhattan.

# The Discovery of Fire

Strictly off-limits, the composing room
trembled with the totems of his craft.
Poker-faced metronome gagged by day,
unbound to tick and chat at night; tuning
fork just *asking* for it; crisp staves
he'd rolled by hand across creamy paper
with the curious tool I raked through butter
and paid for with a shaking and no tea.

Under spots, in frills and velvet dickey,
I kiss the tart mouthpiece and start to tongue
the opening bars of *The Old Rugged Cross*.
As the notes elude me, my ruffled front
combusts, lips solder themselves onto the brass.
They kick my glowing embers from the stage.

# Corrie Sonnet

The closing theme tune scored my bedtimes
with keening inevitability.
"I wish *I'd* written that," would come the line.
"We'd be living in bloody luxury."
But they only paid Eric Spear six quid
for the melody that mourned its way
down ginnels and wash-day alleyways.
"Adn't you best be off to bed, our kid?"
"Why do we watch this rubbish anyway?"
"Dad, it's meant to be the Shakespeare o't soaps."
"I'd rather watch *Pot Black* or *Mash* any day,
I spend enough time wi' ordinary folk.
Mind you, that Elsie Tanner's still gorgeous."
My sister stayed up to watch *The Borgias.*

## Paper Not Loaded

How violently the printer reels
when the ream runs out,
mid-print. Lights flash, gears spin,
catching on nothing, panicking
itself into a paperless abyss.

I think of that sudden dawn,
her stroking your tummy
and the pain lurching into your eyes,
stopping your hearts, ending the day right there
and then.

# Scattered

I'm supposed to kneel to the North Sea now
to pay my respects to your ashes, strewn
so profligately and inaccurately there.
No marker, no buoy, no warning to shipping
that might show me where you are,
and no slot between Dogger and Thames
to forecast how things will be for you.
I wish you were in the peaty earth
of Marsden Moor or Meltham—where,
to shake me off your beery trail, you said
they chopped men's heads off in the square
—caked up in the malt loaf loam
and suety soil, the heart-hugging savour
of all the food you never had as a lad.

# Yuri Gagarin's Three Homecomings

The first man to fall from Heaven to Earth,
ploughing into the soil of April 12th,
1961; the meteoric birth
watched by an old woman, her daughter, their cow.

March 27th, 1968,
pulling out of a steep bank just too late
you assumed the test pilot's frequent fate.

Your orbiting odyssey finally done
on March 23rd, 2001;
in its frame on a wall of the homecoming Mir,
your bright smile melts to gold against atmosphere.

# Desert Orchid

So much abduction, obituary and ossuary
that this long-jaw eye-roll flank-twitch
resignation gives me pause;
makes me long to lie amid the gamey straw
of a blameless life smoked out of nostrils flared
and into the paddock where souls strut,
on-the-muscle, unjockeyed, colourless.

# Bath Time

You like the clear hot water,
flat as glass, into which you
refract your limbs, easing
yourself until the water cuts
you off at the neck, your head
a beautiful prize on a platter
but still blinking, smiling
above invisible coils of essential oil.

I have a more boisterous bent
and sometimes chuck too much bubble bath
under the surging tap and summon
Himalayas of froth, some kind of
Quatermass Experiment in soap
into which I plunge and sculpt
shark fins; Devil's Tower, Wyoming;
the iceberg that snagged the Titanic.

I suggest we bathe together.
"We don't know each other well enough."
I cross fingers for the adverb, "yet."
Your waters are too clear for now,
reveal too much. In the meantime,
let's clothe ourselves in this bubble wrap,
let me work the kinks out of your back.
I'll take the ill-favoured end with the taps.

# Fitting

Traditionally, men will sit nearby in leather seats
or, in cheaper boutiques, on office surplus chairs.
Maybe flipping through *Men's Health* or *FHM*
while wives and girlfriends try things on, with dutiful assistants
pinning hems or sighing Saturday girls clattering hangers
back on racks, snarling with rolling eyes that "There's a queue."
But I pick my angle through the door of the changing room
to watch your naked feet rehearse the dance of sliding in and out
of pants and dresses, shoes and blouses, garments slipping up and down
with now and then a little show-and-tell as you yank the curtain,
reveal with a frown a tightly-waisted purple gown
then back again to just the feet, the turning ankles, balancing acts,
as you crane your neck to see how this or that looks from the back
and even if these things are chosen more with him in mind than me,
I'm held by your displays in proud and silent ecstasies.

## Immuring St Paul's

From my window, just the blazing cross by night,
the dome lost behind Bishopsgate's parade
of gilded atria, hydraulic window-
cleaning turrets. To be expected perhaps.
Progress, you know. Got to keep up with
the upstart bourse in Frankfurt, the changing skylines
of Hong Kong, Tokyo, New York falling
then rallying to close on record highs.
Here on Newgate Street where should be
Wren's great urban umbra, they're bricking
her in again; a heretic or fallen Catholic nun,
Combisafe and Costain vouchsafing her
as executive toy, wallpaper for
PowerPoint presentations, water cooler moments.

## My Best Friend

sees every Iranian flick,
makes tiny notes in caffs,
likes a full English
but not a fried slice
because "fried slice is wrong",
sucks on a pipe full of cotton wool
that I bought him, pissed,
on Seventh Avenue,
dealt with his mum's suicide,
gets to the smallest exhibitions,
makes all technology go wrong,
stood by me when I went mad,
understands Hegel,
reads a lot of S-F,
lives around the corner,
comes to Lambchop gigs,
eats too quickly,
drinks Maker's Mark,
might be leaving town.

# The Hands

An hour hand can roughly mark the time
and prompt us when to eat and work and sleep
and for our daily purpose this is meet
but when are we to dream, create or dine?

To savour life, we need a second hand—
a minute hand, if we're to be precise;
as elegant a pair as man and wife,
these two survey each day and countermand

the carelessness with which we let years pass,
the speed at which the future forms the past.
To moor our hearts beyond the churning tides
it helps to have another mate beside,
for love can coax the chaos to a stop:
both hands on the noon and midnight clock.

*For Andreea and Adam*

# Gyroscope

Poised at (or a suspicion past) my midpoint.
Space junk like this gravity-cheating toy
spins around on an orbit from man to boy
and plucks at the tightrope we both walk.

From Blackpool, with a miniature Tower
from which it leaned at laughable angles
with the plausibility of angels
morris dancing on the point of a pin.

Thrumming along strings, goofing on pencil tip:
just physics, but I thought it magical
and set it on my flattened palm to tickle
a wobble-free path along my life line.

Climbing the ridges of my index finger,
the flywheel in the delicate structure
slows and entropy rushes in like water
to drag the freewheeling memory below.

## Nato e Morto

My Italian is a pocketful
of leftover euros. I use them up,
requesting return *vaporetto* tickets
to the island cemetery of San Michele.

The *bigliettaio* assures us that
it's too soon to take the one-way trip.
Out on the breezy green lagoon, my mother
does her trick with shades and scarf that cuts

her age in half and has waiters mistake us
for husband and wife. The low-lying isle
of the dead drifts towards us.
Once through the portal we find celebrity slabs:

Stravinsky and Diaghilev, Pound obscured
by petals and dust. I place a pebble
on Brodsky's stone, add a biro to the bristling
jar at its base. He'll not be short of a pen

when new ideas come. But we're not here
for photo-ops or grave rubbings.
We came to mingle with the Catholic mass,
to walk where the locals serry

shoulder to shoulder in the soil. We pass
the plots of friars, sisters and soldiers;
so many sailors are wrecked here, their fingers
purchasing just enough to keep them above

the sea that is coming to take it all back.
The dot of the groundsman's tractor grows
from the squint of an avenue's
vanishing point. We see the plume of smoke

before we hear the engine of its steady
approach. A pair of golden ballet shoes
swivel en pointe at the corner of
a sun-bleached lid, alongside (N1982–M1996)

and a photo propped, as if on a table top,
of a black-haired daughter pirouetting
for the local press on the white steps
of Santa Maria della Salute.

Mum has wandered off with a watering can
from the neat metal stand and is sprinkling
some flinching plants and flowers shrinking
from the heat. To reach her I must pass

the freshest pit that looks and smells
like it was dug today and I stand
on the brink and wonder who made up this bed
and who's to lie in it and will it be

a restful night, or is there an adamantine
pea of sin beneath the mattresses
of endless sleep? The tractor buzzes
in my ear; I can see the groundsman's face.

She's found a flotilla of tiny tombs
with baby snaps fading in the sun's
nuclear stare. A crumpled face haloed
by knitted shawl; a hint of the old man

he might have become, but free of the decades
of graven care; his *nato e morto*
wrapped up in one year. "Read this for me."
"*La tua scomparsa così improvvisa*

*mi ha lasciato in uno sconcertante*
*dolore. Aiutami dal cielo*
*come mi hai aiutato in vita.*"
"What did it say?" she asks. "Something like:

the way you were suddenly snatched left me
in bewildering pain. Help me from Heaven
as you helped me in life." The groundsman
has lowered the trailing blades into the beds

and the tractor clatters past this baby Boot Hill
with its milk teeth stones and whole histories
cupped between the palms of a single day.
Cut grass stings our eyes.

The boat ferries back the hundred years
we've amassed and which barely seem to displace
one molecule of water, or persuade
a single green weed to bend as we pass.

## Outlook Good

Another Kentuckian bourbon night's swill
and swell rocks me gently in the dark
as I wait for the nightly shipping forecast
while sailors in oils slick cross deck to hear
their fate from the oracle of Broadcasting House
and long to be cardiganed and coffeed
in Studio B with a black cab waiting
to drive the tarmac miles to sanctuary,
and a single helmsman paws over charts
by the light of a kerosene lamp that swings
and knocks his forehead with each restless turn
of the Atlantic as she takes more
and more duvet for herself and finally
kicks all the brackish green bedclothes to the floor,
and chilled by the six or seven rising
to gale force eight he sets his alarm for fifteen
minutes' time and tries to get his head down,
and wishes he were living in Switzerland
where shipping forecasts are as useful
as pollen warnings on the moon, but
I dream of casting off from the nodding
donkey derrick of Cape Cod with a bait-hold
jammed with slabs of frozen squid and forty miles
of monofilament, hooks, buoys, beepers,
leaders, gaffs and slime knives to dress the throngs
of swordfish I would haul on deck under
waxing moons that never wane in ocean
breaks that furnish forth fish like the pot
that wouldn't stop.